à Madame la Comtesse Greffulhe

Pavane
(avec chœur)

Comte Robert
de Montesquiou-Fézensac

Op. 50

* or **Andante molto moderato** (♩= 84); please see the introductory note.

Printed in Great Britain

OXFORD UNIVERSITY PRESS MUSIC DEPARTMENT
GREAT CLARENDON STREET, OXFORD OX2 6DP • 198 MADISON AVENUE, NEW YORK, NY 10016
The Moral Rights of the Editor have been asserted. Photocopying this copyright material is ILLEGAL.

4

It's Lindor!

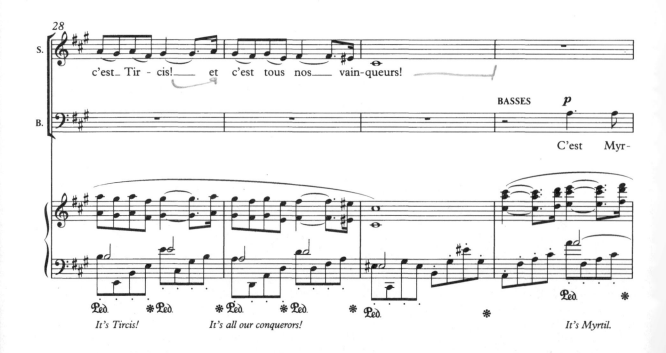

It's Tircis!   It's all our conquerors!   It's Myrtil.

6

presume to reign over our fates and our lives!

Watch out!

* Bars 47–48 assigned to sopranos in autograph.

Keep time!

Oh, the mortal

insult!   The cadence is less slow

and the fall more certain.   We shall

and so it is always!   *We love each other!*   *We hate each other!*

We curse our loves!

On mau-dit ses a-mours!

A-dieu Myr-

Farewell

-til!___ É - glé!___ Chlo - é! dé - mons mo-

Myrtil! Egle! Chloe! Mocking

A - - dieu donc et bons jours

-queurs!

demons! Farewell then and good days

12

to the tyrants of our hearts!

And farewell!

ISBN 0-19-341818-5

Printed and bound in Great Britain by
Halstan & Co. Ltd., Amersham, Bucks